SPACE ENCYCLOPEDIA

SATELLITES

Om KIDZ

An imprint of **Om** Books International

Contents

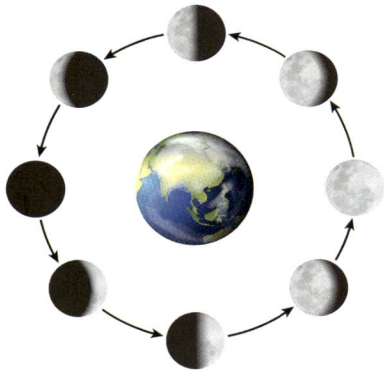

SATELLITES

It has been found that about 168 natural satellites orbit around the planets of the solar system.

▲ *It has been found that about 168 natural satellites orbit around the planets of the solar system.*

A satellite can be a moon, planet or machine that orbits a planet or star. For example, planet Earth is a satellite since it orbits the Sun. And, the moon is a satellite because it orbits Earth. ''Satellite'' is a word that is often used to refer to a machine launched into space and orbits Earth or another body in space.

Several artificial or human-made satellites orbit Earth. Some take pictures of the planet that help meteorologists predict weather and track hurricanes, while others take pictures of other planets, the Sun, black holes, dark matter or faraway galaxies. These pictures help scientists to better understand the solar system and the universe.

Earth's Moon

The moon is Earth's only natural satellite. Although not the largest natural satellite in the solar system, it is the largest among the satellites of major planets that is relative to the size of the object it orbits. The moon is a cold, rocky body that is about 3,476 km in diameter. It does not have a light of its own, but shines by the sunlight reflected from its surface.

Earth came first

The moon is thought to have formed nearly 4.5 billion years ago, not long after Earth. Although there have been several hypotheses behind its origin in the past, the current most widely accepted explanation is that the moon formed from the debris that was left over after a giant impact between Earth and a Mars-sized body named Theia.

Internal structure

The moon has a distinct crust, mantle and core. It has a very small core that consists of only one to two per cent of the total mass and is roughly 680 km wide. It mostly consists of iron, but may also contain large amounts of sulphur and other elements. Its rocky mantle

Moon surface ▼

is about 1,330 km thick and made up of dense rocks that are rich in iron and magnesium. The crust on top is about 70 km deep. The outermost part of the crust is broken because of the large impacts it has received, a shattered zone that gives way to intact material below a depth of about 9.6 km.

Moon's atmosphere

The moon has a very thin atmosphere, so a layer of dust can sit undisturbed for centuries. Heat is not held near the surface without much of an atmosphere, so temperatures vary heavily. Temperatures range from 134 °C to -153 °C.

Gravity

The moon has a much weaker gravity than Earth, due to its smaller mass, so one would weigh about one-sixth (16.5%) of their weight on Earth.

Phases of the moon

One moon rotation lasts for the same amount of time that it takes to orbit Earth and therefore the same side faces us. While it is orbiting, its appearance keeps changing as sunlight falls on

different areas on its surface. While in orbit, the side where sunlight falls reduces and then grows. When it faces the Sun, it is fully lit up. We refer to this event as the full moon. These changes in appearance are referred to as phases. It takes 29 and a half days to complete an entire cycle of these phases.

Phases of Earth's moon.

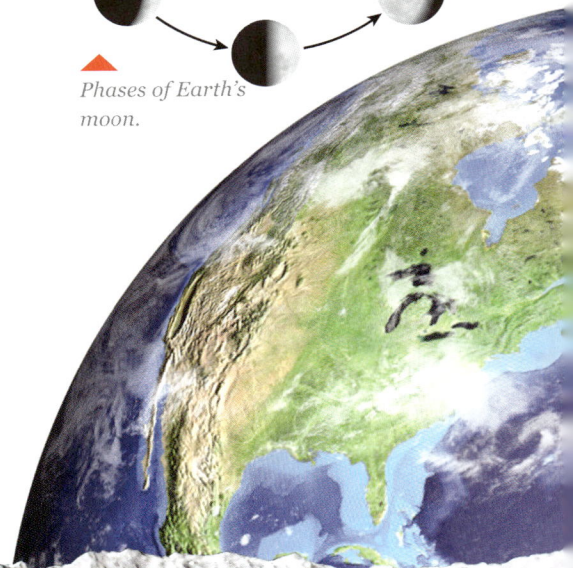

Moon's soil

The moon's surface is covered by a mud-like layer that is several metres thick. On the moon's surface, this mud-like substance is fine. As you go deeper, the size of the particles starts getting much bigger. Solid rock lies at a depth of about 16.4 feet down on the moon and the soil is 32.8 feet deep in the mountainous regions. Asteroids hitting the moon's surface resulted in soil getting formed at a rate of 20 km per second. As a result, the rock got squashed and craters were produced.

Moon's surface

The moon's surface took form a few years after it came into existence. A few billion years of continuous asteroid showers were followed by volcanic welling up from the moon's interior and filling low-lying regions. The spots that we see on the moon from Earth are the craters that are formed by asteroid collisions.

The blue moon

According to modern folklore, a blue moon is the second full moon in a calendar month. In a month there is only one full moon. However, a second one could also occur. Full moons occur after a 29 days cycle, whereas most months consist of 30 or 31 days. Therefore, two full moons can appear in a single month. This phenomenon occurs every two and a half years, on average.

Is the moon really blue?

The date of a full moon does not affect the moon's colour. The moon on 31st July is usually pearly-grey. Interestingly there was a time, not long ago, when people saw blue moons almost every night. Full moons, half moons and crescent moons were all blue. On some nights, they would be green.

Why does it turn blue?

In 1883, an Indonesian volcano named Krakatoa exploded. Scientists equate the blast to a 100-megaton nuclear bomb. Plumes of ash rose to the very top of Earth's atmosphere, making the moon turn blue. Krakatoa's ash is the reason for the blue moon. White moonbeams shining through the clouds emerged blue and occasionally green. Blue moons lasted for years after the eruption. Other less potent volcanoes have turned the moon blue as well. Blue moons were also observed in 1983 after the eruption of the El Chichon volcano in Mexico. There are reports of blue moons caused by Mt St. Helens in 1980 and Mt Pinatubo in 1991 as well.

Moon is the second-densest satellite among those whose densities are known.

Lunar Eclipse

A lunar eclipse occurs when the moon passes directly behind Earth into its umbra (shadow). This can occur only when the Sun, Earth and moon are aligned exactly with Earth in the middle. Hence, a lunar eclipse can only occur on the night of a full moon.

Types of lunar eclipse

A penumbral eclipse occurs when the moon passes through Earth's penumbra. The penumbra causes a subtle darkening of the moon's surface. A special type of penumbral eclipse is a total penumbral eclipse, during which the moon lies exclusively within Earth's penumbra. Total penumbral eclipses are rare and when these occur, that portion of the moon that is closest to the umbra can appear somewhat darker than the rest of the moon. A partial lunar eclipse occurs when only a portion of the moon enters the umbra.

When the moon travels completely into Earth's umbra, one observes a total lunar eclipse and it may last up to nearly 107 minutes.

However, the total time between the moon's first and last contact with the shadow is much longer and could last up to four hours.

Lunar eclipse.

Horizontal eclipse

A selenelion or selenehelion occurs when both the Sun and eclipsed moon can be simultaneously observed. This can only happen either before sunset or after sunrise. Both these bodies will appear just above the horizon at nearly opposite points in the sky. This arrangement has led to the phenomenon being referred to as a horizontal eclipse. Although the moon is in Earth's umbra, the Sun and eclipsed moon can both be seen at the same time because the refraction of light through Earth's atmosphere causes each of them to appear higher in the sky than their true geometric position.

Unlike a solar eclipse, lunar eclipses are safe to view without any special precautions, as they are dimmer than the full moon.

FUN FACT

Unlike a solar eclipse, which can only be viewed from a certain relatively small area of the world, a lunar eclipse may be viewed from anywhere on the night side of Earth. A lunar eclipse lasts for a few hours, whereas a total solar eclipse lasts for only a few minutes at any given place due to the smaller size of the moon's shadow.

Timing

The timing of a total lunar eclipse is determined by its contacts:

First contact: Beginning of the penumbral eclipse. Earth's penumbra touches the moon's outer limb.

Second contact: Beginning of the partial eclipse. Earth's umbra touches the moon's outer limb.

Third contact: Beginning of the total eclipse. The moon's surface is entirely within Earth's umbra.

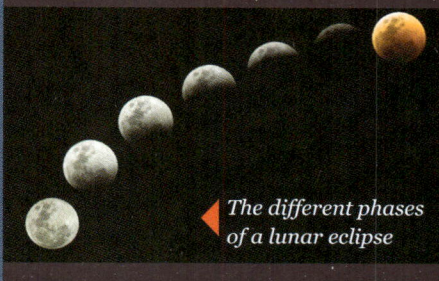

◀ *The different phases of a lunar eclipse*

Greatest eclipse: The peak stage of the total eclipse. The moon is at its closest to the centre of Earth's umbra.

Fourth contact: End of the total eclipse. The moon's outer limb exits Earth's umbra.

Fifth contact: End of the partial eclipse. Earth's umbra leaves the moon's surface.

Sixth contact: End of the penumbral eclipse. Earth's penumbra no longer makes contact with the moon.

Numerous early civilisations utilised the Moon's monthly cycle to quantify the passage of time. In fact, some calendars are synchronised to the phases of the moon. The Hebrew, Muslim and Chinese calendars are all lunar calendars.

Blood moon

Due to its reddish colour, a totally eclipsed moon is sometimes referred to as a ''blood moon''. The most recent blood moon occurred on 8th October, 2014, and was visible across much of the Americas and Asia.

Lunar versus solar eclipse

There is often confusion between a solar and lunar eclipse. While both involve interactions between the Sun, Earth and moon, they are very different in their interactions. The moon does not completely disappear as it passes through the umbra because of the refraction of sunlight by Earth's atmosphere into the shadow cone. If Earth had no atmosphere, the moon would be completely dark during an eclipse. The red colouring arises because the sunlight reaching the moon must pass through a long and dense layer of Earth's atmosphere, where it is scattered.

A solar eclipse occurs in the day time at new moon, when the moon is between Earth and the Sun, while a lunar eclipse occurs at night when Earth passes between the Sun and the moon.
▼

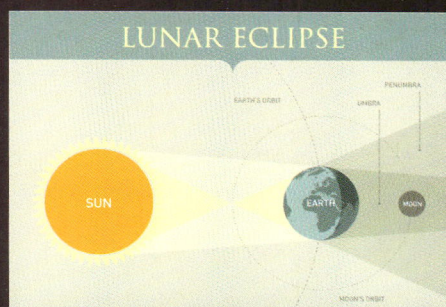

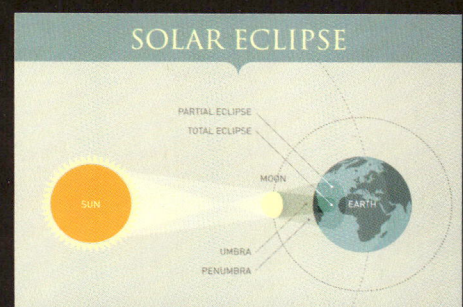

LUNAR ECLIPSE

SOLAR ECLIPSE

Lunar Tides

The moon's gravity pulls at Earth, causing predictable rises and falls in sea levels known as "tides". High tides are when water bulges upward and low tides are when water drops down. High tides result on the side of Earth that is nearest to the moon due to gravity. It also happens on the side farthest from the moon due to the inertia of water. Low tides occur between these two tidal humps.

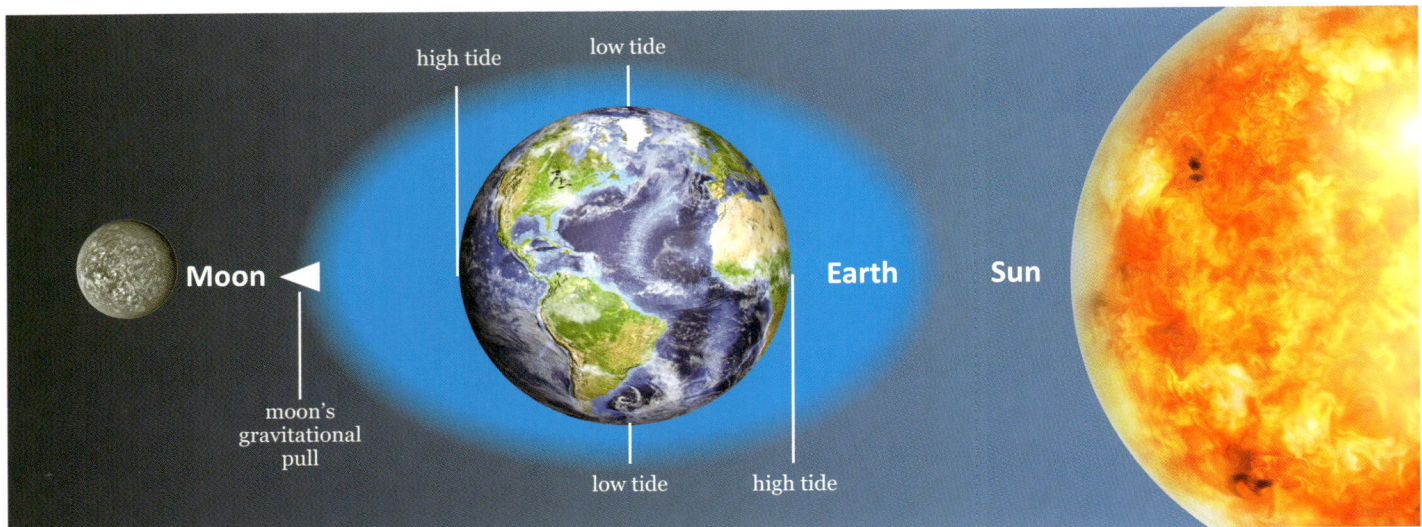

▲ *Illustration showing Earth, moon and tidal influence.*

The moon moves

The energy that Earth loses is picked up by the moon, increasing its distance from Earth, which means that the moon moves farther away by 3.8 cm annually.

Lunar eclipses

During eclipses, the moon, Earth and Sun are in a straight line, or nearly so. A lunar eclipse occurs when Earth gets directly or almost directly between the Sun and moon, and Earth's shadow falls on the moon.

A lunar eclipse can occur only during a full moon. A solar eclipse occurs when the moon gets directly or nearly directly between the Sun and Earth, and the moon's shadow falls on it. A solar eclipse can occur only during a new moon.

Effects of the Sun

The Sun also has an effect on the tidal timings of the oceans on Earth. The Sun has a gravitational force that keeps the entire solar system revolving around it. It is bound to exert a certain amount of gravitational pull on the water bodies on Earth. The Sun's gravity also causes tides. However, since the distance between the Sun and Earth is almost 400 times the distance between the moon and Earth, the force of gravity exerted on Earth's water is very less as compared to the force of the moon's gravity. For example, the tides that are formed in Tahiti are due to the Sun's gravity and are of lower amplitude.

An artist's representation of the moon affecting the tides. ▼

FUN FACT

The word "month" is derived from the moon's 29.5-day period of orbit around Earth. The phases of the moon are tracked on a lunar calendar and is different from the Georgian calendar.

Martian Moons

Mars has two moons, Phobos and Deimos, which are thought to be captured asteroids. Both satellites were discovered in 1877 by Asaph Hall. It is possible that Mars may have moons smaller than 50–100 m and a dust ring between Phobos and Deimos may be present, but none have been discovered yet.

Etymology

The names are based on the characters Phobos (fear) and Deimos (terror) who, in Greek mythology, accompanied their father Ares, god of war, into battle. Ares was known as Mars to the Romans. The motions of Phobos and Deimos would appear very different from that of our own moon. Speedy Phobos rises in the west, sets in the east and rises again in just 11 hours, while Deimos, being only just outside the synchronous orbit, rises as expected in the east, but very slowly.

Captured asteroids

The origin of the Martian moons is still controversial. Based on their similarity, one hypothesis is that both moons

Both moons are tidally locked, always presenting the same face towards Mars.

may be captured main-belt asteroids. Both sets of findings support an origin of Phobos from material ejected by an impact on Mars that re-accreted in the Martian orbit, similar to the prevailing theory for the origin of Earth's moon.

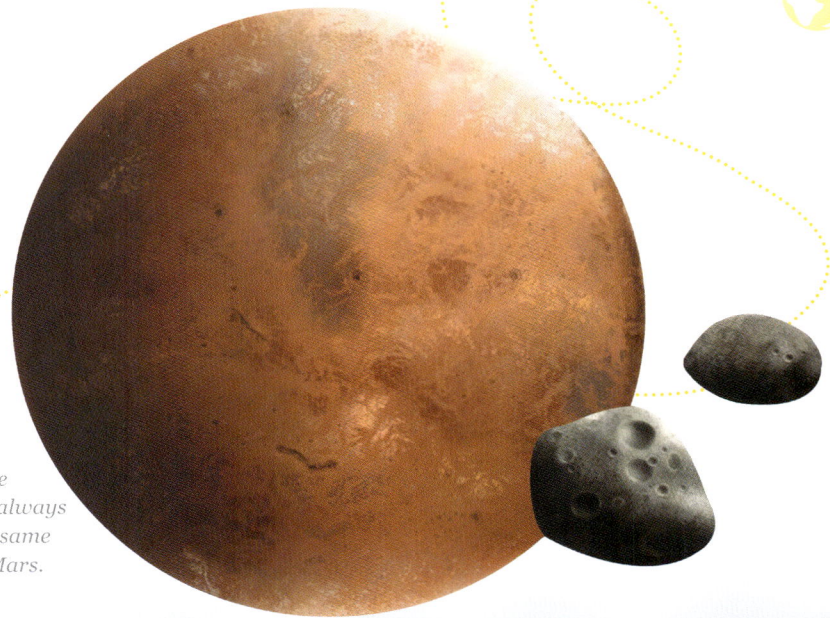

However, both, Phobos and Deimos resemble asteroids more than moons.

Dimensions

Phobos is larger than Deimos and is 22 km in diameter. The smaller moon Deimos is only 13 km wide. This makes them both two of the smallest moons in the solar system.

FUN FACT

Phobos is so small that although it is closer to Mars as compared to any other moon and its planet, it only looks one-third the size of our moon when observed from Mars.

Phobos

Phobos (Mars I) is the larger and closer of the two natural satellites of Mars. Both moons were discovered in 1877. A small, irregularly shaped object with a mean radius of 11 km, it is seven times more massive than Mars's outer moon, Deimos.
It is named after the Greek god Phobos, son of Ares (Mars) and Aphrodite (Venus), which was the personification of horror.

shaped surface. The grooves are typically less than 30 m deep, 100–200 m wide and up to 20 km long.

The unique Kaidun meteorite is thought to be a piece of Phobos but this has been difficult to verify since little is known about the detailed composition of the moon.

Predicted destruction

Tidal deceleration is gradually decreasing the orbital radius of Phobos. Observations of Phobos's orbit leads to the conclusion that it will be destroyed

The moon Phobos

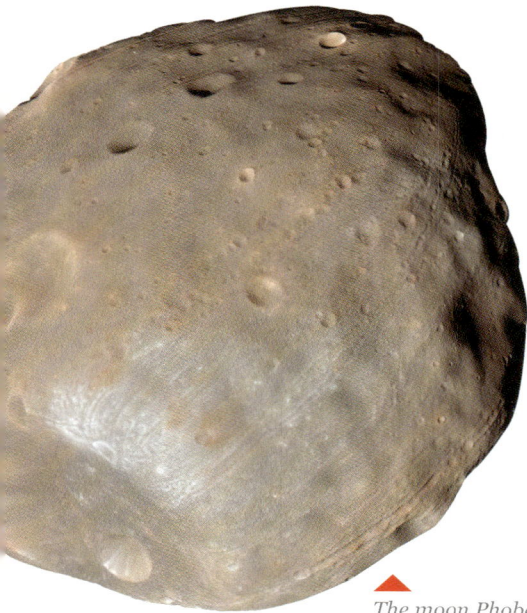
Phobos and Deimos orbiting around Mars.

Appearance

Phobos is too small to be rounded under its own gravity. It does not have an atmosphere due to low mass and gravity. It is one of the least reflective bodies in the solar system. Its density is too low to be a solid rock and is known to have significant porosity.

Stickney crater

It is heavily cratered. The most prominent surface feature is the crater called Stickney, named after Asaph Hall's wife, Angeline Stickney Hall, Stickney being her maiden name. The impact that created Stickney must have nearly shattered Phobos. Many grooves and streaks also cover the oddly

An artist's representation of the planet Mars along with one of its moons, Phobos, orbiting around it.

in less than 30–50 million years. Given its irregular shape and assuming that it is a Mohr–Coulomb body, it will eventually break up when it reaches approximately 2.1 Mars radii.

FUN FACT

It is speculated that Phobos is hollow due to its unusual orbital characteristics.

Deimos

Deimos (Mars II) is the smaller and farther of the two natural satellites of Mars with a mean radius of 6.2 km, the other being Phobos. Deimos takes 30.3 hours to orbit Mars. In Greek mythology, Deimos is Phobos's twin brother. It means "terror".

They resemble asteroids more than the moons of the planet Mars.

orbits, which lie almost exactly in Mars's equatorial plane.

FUN FACT

At its brightest, i.e., "full moon", it would be about as bright as Venus is from Earth.

Solar transits

It regularly passes in front of the Sun. It is too small to cause a total eclipse, appearing only as a small black dot moving across the Sun. On 4th March, 2004, a transit of Deimos was photographed by Mars Rover Opportunity and on 13th March, 2004, a transit was photographed by Mars Rover Spirit.

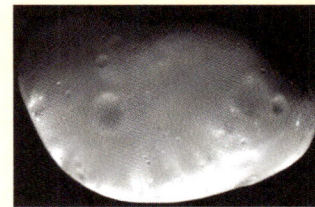

The Deimos looks like a smaller irregular moon.

The discovery

Based on the fact that Earth has a moon and Jupiter has four, Johannes Kepler suggested years ago that it was very possible for Mars to have atleast two moons. However, it wasn't till years later that Asaph Hall, after researching the area carefully and focus searching Mars' moons, discovered them on 12th August, 1877.

Deimos, the smaller moon of Mars.

Appearance

Like most bodies of its size, it is highly non-spherical and half the size of Phobos. It is composed of rock that is rich in carbonaceous materials. It is cratered, but the surface is noticeably smoother than that of Phobos, caused by the partial filling of craters with regolith (a layer of loose, heterogeneous material covering solid rock). The regolith is highly porous. The two largest craters, Swift and Voltaire, each measure about 3 km across.

Orbits of Phobos and Deimos

Deimos' orbit is nearly circular and close to Mars' equatorial plane. Deimos, Mars' outer moon, is possibly an asteroid that was perturbed by Jupiter into an orbit that allowed it to be captured by Mars. Both Deimos and Phobos have very circular

Jovian moons

Jupiter has a total of 67 known moons, including four large moons known as the Galilean satellites. This almost qualifies it as another solar system. Its size plays a role in the number of moons orbiting it because there is a large area of gravitational stability around it to support many moons.

Orbital periods

The moons of Jupiter have orbital periods ranging from seven hours to almost three Earth years. Some of the orbits are nearly circular, while the moons farthest from Jupiter have more irregular orbits.

Galilean moons

Most of Jupiter's moons are small, which is less than 9.7 km in diameter. In January 1610, Italian astronomer Galileo Galilee discovered four of Jupiter's moons—now called Io, Europa, Ganymede and Callisto. He originally referred to the individual moons numerically as I, II, III and IV. Eight satellites—the four Galilean and four smaller moons—are closer to the planet and provide the dust that make up Jupiter's rings.

After alternatively using Roman names and numerals to address the moons of Jupiter that were discovered one after another, the IAU finally decided on a specific mean of nomenclature. In 1975, they decided to name the newly discovered moons after the lovers and favourites, and later according to the names of the daughters of Jupiter. Out of the 67 moons of Jupiter, moon number 66 has been named Megaclite and moon 67 still has to be named.

Jupiter was named after the mythological character Io, a priestess of Hera who became one of his lovers.

Jupiter and the four Galilean satellites.

The four Galilean moons orbiting around Jupiter.

FUN FACT

The Galilean moons are by far the largest and most massive objects in the orbit around Jupiter, with the remaining 63 moons and rings together comprising just 0.003 per cent of the total orbiting mass.

Io

Io is the innermost of the four Galilean moons of Jupiter. It is the fourth-largest moon. It has the highest density among all the moons and is the driest known object in the solar system.

Geologically active object

With over 400 active volcanoes, Io is the most geologically active object in the solar system. This extreme activity is because of tidal heating from friction that is generated within Io's interior as it is pulled between Jupiter and the other Galilean satellites—Europa, Ganymede and Callisto.

Several volcanoes produce plumes of sulphur and sulphur dioxide that climb as high as 500 km above the surface. Io's surface is also dotted with more than 100 mountains that have been uplifted by extensive compression at the base of Io's silicate crust. Some of these peaks are even taller than Mount Everest.

A representation of an artificial satellite capturing the image of Jupiter's moons.

Volcanoes

Io's volcanism is responsible for many of its unique features. Its volcanic plumes and flowing lava produce large surface changes. They paint the surface in various subtle shades of yellow, red, white, black and green, largely due to allotropes and compounds of sulphur.

Numerous extensive streams of lava, more than 500 km in length, also mark the surface. The materials produced by this volcanism make up Io's thin, patchy atmosphere and Jupiter's extensive magnetosphere. Io's volcanic ejecta (the particles ejected from a volcano) also produce a large plasma torus (the ring) around Jupiter.

FUN FACT

Besides Earth, Io is the only known body in the solar system to have observed active volcanoes.

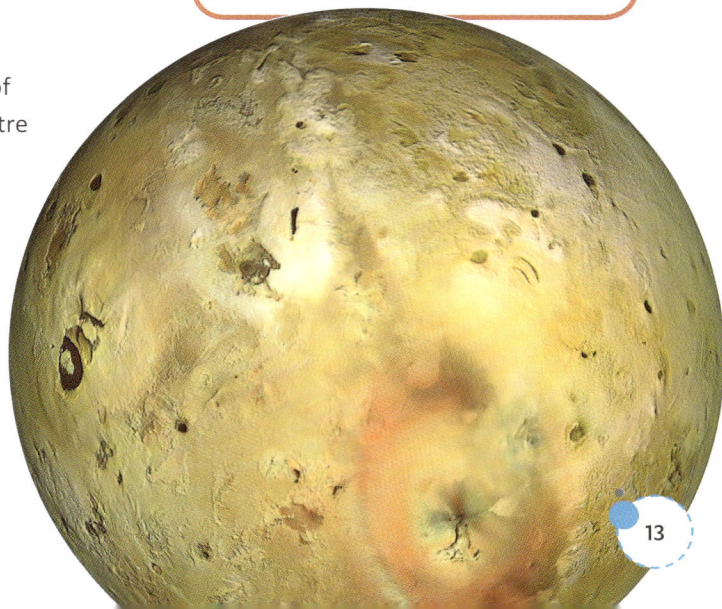

Rotation and revolution

Io orbits Jupiter at a distance of 421,700 km from Jupiter's centre and 350,000 km from its cloud tops. Its orbit lies between those of Thebe and Europa. Including Jupiter's inner satellites, Io is the fifth moon out from Jupiter.

Comparison between Jupiter and its moons.

13

Europa

Europa (Jupiter II) is the sixth-closest moon of Jupiter and the smallest of its four Galilean satellites. But it is still the sixth-largest moon in the solar system. Like all the Galilean satellites, Europa is named after a lover of Zeus (the Greek counterpart of Jupiter), after the daughter of the king of Tyre.

Rotation and revolution

Europa takes almost four days to orbit Jupiter. Like its fellow Galilean satellites, it is tidally locked to Jupiter, with one hemisphere of Europa constantly facing Jupiter like Earth's moon.

Appearance

Europa is slightly smaller than the moon. At just over 3,100 km in diameter, it is the sixth-largest moon and 15th largest object in the solar system. However, by a wide margin, it is the least massive of the Galilean satellites. Nonetheless, it is comparatively larger than all the known moons in the solar system.

Internal structure

Europa has an outer layer of water around 100 km thick; some as frozen ice above the crust and some as liquid ocean beneath the ice.

Geological structures

Europa is one of the smoothest objects in the solar system. However, its equator has been thought to be covered in 10 m tall icy spikes called "penitents". These are formed by the effect of direct overhead sunlight on the equator and melting vertical cracks. Its most striking surface features are a series of dark streaks crisscrossing the entire globe, called "lineae". The edges of its crust on either side of the cracks have moved relatively to each other.

A series of dark lines known as lineae are seen across the surface of Europa.

FUN FACT

The radiation level at the surface of Europa is sufficiently high, resulting in severe illness or even death in human beings, who are exposed to it even for a single day!

Subsurface ocean

Scientists believe that a layer of liquid water exists beneath Europa's surface. It is the heat from tidal flexing that allows the subsurface ocean to remain liquid.

The larger bands are more than 20 km across, often with dark, diffused outer edges, regular striations and a central band of lighter material.

Ganymede

Ganymede (Jupiter III) is Jupiter's satellite. It is the largest moon in the solar system. It has a diameter of 5,268 km, eight per cent larger than Mercury, but has only 45 per cent of its mass. Its diameter is two per cent larger than Saturn's Titan, the second largest moon. It also has the highest mass of all planetary satellites, with 2.02 times the mass of Earth's moon. It is the seventh moon and third Galilean satellite on the outer side of Jupiter, orbiting at about 1.070 million km. It takes Ganymede about seven Earth days to orbit Jupiter.

Tidal lock

Ganymede orbits Jupiter at a distance of 1,070,400 km. It is third among the Galilean satellites and completes a revolution every seven days and three hours. Like most known moons, Ganymede is tidally locked, with one side always facing towards the planet.

Composition

Its average density suggests a composition of approximately equal parts rocky material and water, which is mainly ice. Some additional volatile ices such as ammonia may also be present.

Internal structure

It appears to be fully differentiated, consisting of an iron sulphide – iron core and silicate mantle. The precise thicknesses of the different layers in its interior depend on the assumed composition of silicates and a small amount of sulphur in the core.

Accretion of Ganymede

Ganymede was probably formed by an accretion in Jupiter's sub-nebula, a disc of gas and dust surrounding Jupiter after its formation. The accretion of Ganymede probably took about 10,000 years.

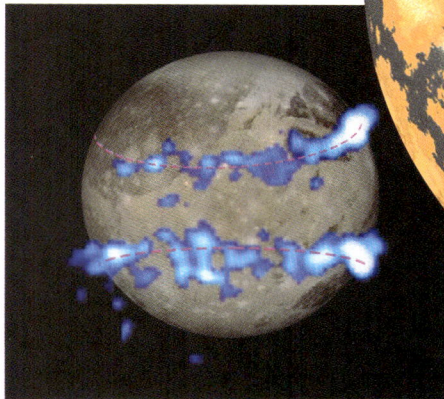

Scientists have observed oceanic movements on the surface of Ganymede through the Hubble Telescope.

Ganymede is the only Galilean moon of Jupiter named after a male figure, like Io, Europa and Callisto. He was a lover of Zeus.

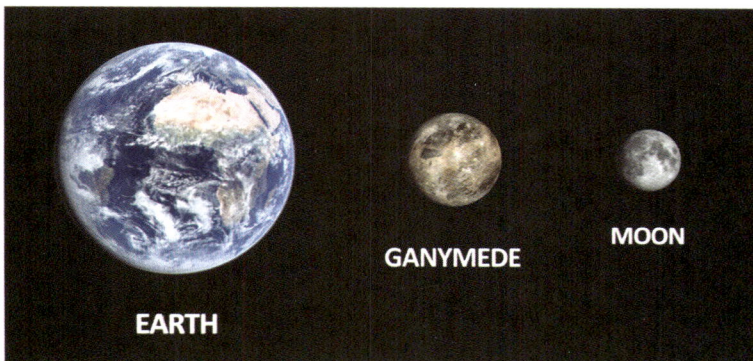

Ganymede compared with Earth and the moon.

EARTH   GANYMEDE   MOON

FUN FACT

Larger than Mercury and Pluto, and only slightly smaller than Mars, Ganymede would easily be classified as a planet if it were orbiting the Sun rather than Jupiter.

Callisto

Callisto (Jupiter IV) is the most heavily cratered object in the solar system. It also has the oldest landscape. It is the outermost of the Galilean moons and has the lowest density compared to the four. It was named after the daughter of the King of Arcadia, Lycaon, who was a companion of Artemis, the hunting goddess.

Orbit

Like other moons, its rotation is locked in order to be synchronous with its orbit. The length of a Callistoan day and its orbital period is about 16.7 days. It also experiences less tidal influences than other Galilean moons because it orbits beyond Jupiter's main radiation belt.

Surface structure

Its surface is the oldest in the solar system. It does not show any signs that geological activity in general have ever occurred on it. It is thought to have evolved predominantly under the influence of impacts. Prominent surface features include multi-ring structures, variously shaped impact craters and chains of craters (catenae), and associated scarps, ridges and deposits. The absolute ages of the landforms are not known.

Callisto is roughly the same size as Mercury. It is the third largest moon in the entire solar system and the second largest in the Jovian system, after Ganymede.

Darkest surface structure

While craters are its signature feature, its surface colouring is also the darkest of all the Galilean moons. Its composition consists of magnesium and iron-bearing hydrated silicates, carbon dioxide, sulphur dioxide and possibly ammonia and other organic compounds. It also consists of equal amounts of rocks and ices.

The crust and the interiors of the Galilean moon Callisto.

The cratered surface of Callisto is known to be one of its distinguished features.

It is thought to be a long dead world, with hardly any geologic activity on its surface.

FUN FACT

The likely presence of an ocean within Callisto leaves a possibility that it could harbour life. Because of its low radiation levels, it has long been considered as the most suitable place for a human base for future exploration of the Jovian system.

Saturn's Moons

The moons of Saturn are several and diverse, ranging from tiny moonlets less than one km across to the gigantic Titan, which is larger than Mercury. Saturn has 62 moons with established orbits, 53 of which have names.

Discovery of the moons

Christiaan Huygens discovered the first known moon of Saturn in 1655 and it was Titan. Giovanni Domenico Cassini made the next four discoveries: Iapetus (1671), Rhea (1672), Dione (1684) and Tethys (1684). William Herschel discovered Mimas and Enceladus in 1789. The next two discoveries came at intervals of 50 or more years: Hyperion in 1848 and Phoebe in 1898.

Saturn's orbit

Saturn has 24 regular satellites; they have orbits not greatly inclined to Saturn's equatorial plane. They include the seven major satellites, four small moons that exist in a Trojan orbit with larger moons and two mutually co-orbital moons.

Irregular moon

The regular satellites are conventionally named after Titans and Titanesses associated with the mythological Saturn. The irregular satellites have been classified by their orbital characteristics into the Inuit, Norse and Gallic groups. Their names are chosen from the corresponding mythologies. The biggest irregular moon is Phoebe, the ninth moon of Saturn, which was discovered at the end of the nineteenth century. This moon belongs to the Norse group and like the rest of the moons in that group, its rotation is retrograde. The surface of Phoebe is scarred by approximately 130 craters, each one about 10 km wide. This moon is the source of the material required for the largest ring around Saturn.

The Saturnian moon system is very unbalanced. The other six ellipsoidal moons constitute roughly four per cent of the mass in orbit around the planet Saturn, while the remaining 55 small moons, with the rings, comprise only 0.04 per cent of it.

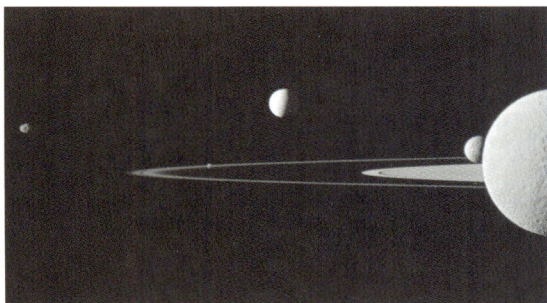

▲ *Saturn along with its satellites in space.*

◀ *Titan comprises more than 96 per cent of the mass in orbit around the planet.*

◀ *Phoebe contributes the material that is required to replenish the biggest ring around Saturn.*

Titan

Titan (Saturn VI) is Saturn's largest moon. It is the only known moon to have a dense atmosphere. It is also the only object besides Earth, where clear evidence of stable bodies of surface liquid has been found. It is the sixth ellipsoidal moon from Saturn. It was the first known moon of Saturn and the fifth known satellite of another planet.

Titan has an atmosphere thicker than Earth's.

Atmosphere

Titan's atmospheric composition in the stratosphere is 98.4 per cent nitrogen and 1.6 per cent of methane and hydrogen. There are trace amounts of other hydrocarbons, such as ethane, diacetylene, methylacetylene and other gases.

Geological structures

The surface of Titan has been described as "complex, fluid-processed and geologically young". It has streaky features, some of them hundreds of kilometres in length, which seem to be caused by windblown rocky particles.

The surface is fairly smooth; the few objects that seem to be impact craters appear to have been filled in, perhaps by raining hydrocarbons or volcanoes.

Its surface is marked by broad regions of bright and dark terrain. The convoluted region is filled with hills and cut by valleys and chasms.

Large areas of Titan's surface are covered with sand dunes made of hydrocarbon. Dunes on Titan may resemble those of the Namibian desert in Africa.

Rotation and revolution

Titan orbits Saturn once every 15 days and 22 hours. Its rotational period is identical to its orbital period. Titan is, thus, tidally locked in synchronous rotation with its host and always shows one face to the planet.

A comparison between Earth, its moon and Saturn's moon Titan.

Saturn's system

It is believed that Saturn's system began with a group of moons similar to Jupiter's Galilean satellites, but they were disrupted by a series of giant impacts, which would go on to form Titan.

A representation of the surface of Titan.

Porous icy crust

Alkanofer in porous icy crust

Expanding clathrate layer in porous icy crust

Non-porous icy crust

Iapetus

Iapetus is the third-largest moon of Saturn, and eleventh-largest in the solar system. It was discovered by Giovanni Cassini in 1672. He first spotted the moon on the west side of the planet, but when he tried to observe it days later on the eastern side, he could not spot it. This led him to surmise that the moon was tidally locked, with one face darker than the other.

Appearance

Unlike most of the moons, Iapetus has a bulging equator and compressed poles. It has low density and is known to be composed primarily of water, with fewer rocks.

A series of high mountains encircle the equator, going more than halfway around the moon. The ridge stretches more than 1,300 km around the moon's circumference. Some of the peaks reach heights of more than 20 km. They are among the highest mountains in the solar system. Iapetus is heavily cratered, and atleast five of these craters are over 350 km wide. The widest crater, Turgis, has a diameter of 580 km. Its rim is extremely steep and includes a scarp about 15 km high.

Two-faced moon

The most striking feature of Iapetus is its dual colouration. The leading hemisphere of the satellite is coal-black, while its rear is brighter. When the moon is facing Earth, its dark leading side keeps it hidden. The coal black region is called Cassini Regio, after the Italian astronomer. One theory suggests that eruptions of dark hydrocarbons from ice volcanoes could have caused the differentiation.

An image showing the bright trailing hemisphere, with part of the dark area appearing on the right. The large crater Engelier is near the bottom.

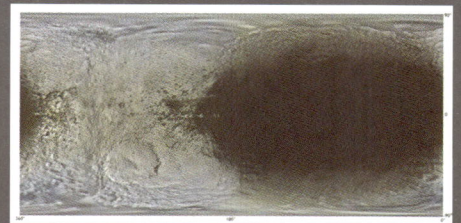

An image providing a closer look at the dark side of Iapetus, that helps it hide when observing from Earth.

An image showing the dark Cassini Region and its border with the bright Roncevaux Terra, Turgis, the largest crater, on the right, and the equatorial ridge.

FUN FACT

Temperature ranges from -143 °C on the warmer dark side to -173 °C on the bright side, which absorbs less heat and is cooler.

Rhea

Rhea is the second-largest moon of Saturn and the ninth-largest moon in the solar system. It is the smallest body in the solar system established in hydrostatic equilibrium. It is the second largest moon of Saturn, resembling a dirty snowball of rock and ice. It is the only moon that has oxygen in its atmosphere. Even though it is thin, it is one of the most heavily cratered satellites in the solar system.

Virtual image of Rhea, named after the Titan Rheaww of Greek mythology, "mother of the gods". It is also designated as Saturn V.

Appearance

It has a density that is 1.233 times that of liquid water, which implies that it is three-quarters ice and one-quarter rock. Rhea has two huge impact basins on its hemisphere. They are between 400 and 500 km across. The northern of the two is called "Tirawa".

Rhea's surface

Its surface can be divided into two different areas based on crater density: the first area contains craters, which are larger than 40 km in diameter while the second area, in parts of the polar and equatorial regions, has craters less than 40 km. The leading hemisphere is heavily cratered and uniformly bright. As a result, Saturn's gravitational pull is less effective on the moon.

Atmosphere

A very faint oxygen atmosphere exists around it, the first direct evidence of an oxygen atmosphere on a body besides Earth. The main source of oxygen is radiolysis of water and ice at the surface by ions supplied by the magnetosphere of Saturn.

In addition to the oxygen, carbon dioxide has also been found in traces, which indicates that it is possible for life to exist on this heavenly body. It has been suggested that the air on Rhea might be breatheable for humans.

There is an impact crater that is prominent because of an extended system of bright rays, called "Inktomi", and is nicknamed "The Splat".

Earth, its moon and Saturn's moon Rhea.

FUN FACT

The atmosphere around Rhea is so thin that oxygen is around five trillion times less dense than that found on Earth!

Dione

Dione, a moon of Saturn, was discovered by Italian astronomer Giovanni Domenico Cassini in 1684. It is named after the Titaness Dione of Greek mythology. It is also designated as Saturn IV. Its orbital period is one-tenth of the moon.

An artist's representation of Dione in comparison to the other moons of Saturn.

Fractures dividing older craters on Dione. The ones running from upper right to lower left are the Carthage Fossae, while Pactolus Catena runs more horizontally on the lower right.

Appearance

Dione is the 15th largest moon in the solar system. It is composed primarily of water ice, but since it is the third densest moon of Saturn, it has denser material like silicate rock in its interior. It has similar albedo features and terrain as Rhea. Both these have dissimilar leading and trailing hemispheres. Its leading hemisphere is cratered and homogeneously bright. Its trailing hemisphere contains a network of bright ice cliffs, which is a distinctive surface feature.

The ice cliffs

Photographs of Dione show wispy features covering its trailing hemisphere. The origin of these features is puzzling, as all that was known was that the material has a high albedo and is sufficiently thin so that it cannot hide the surface beneath. Studies revealed that the wisps were, in fact, not deposits but rather bright ice cliffs created by tectonic fractures.

Dione as seen from Voyager 1; the craters on the upper and lower left are Dido and Aeneas.

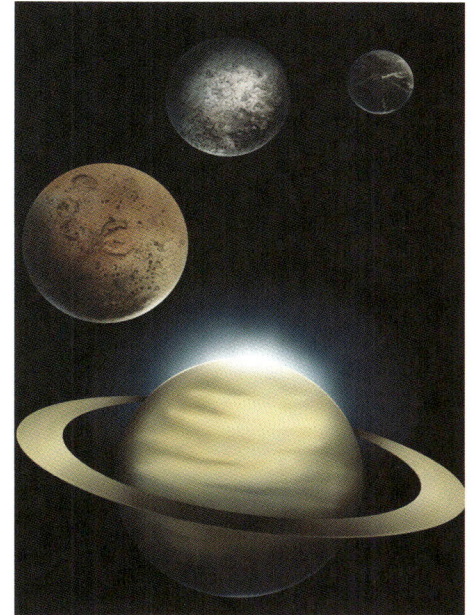

Craters

Dione's surface includes a heavily cratered terrain, fairly cratered plains, lightly cratered plains and areas of tectonic fractures. The heavily cratered terrain has several craters that are larger than 100 km in diameter. The plain areas have craters less than 30 km in diameter. The heavily cratered terrain is located on the trailing hemisphere, while the less cratered plains are present on the leading hemisphere.

FUN FACT

Dione has two Trojan moons, Helene and Polydeuces, which are located within its Lagrangian points L4 and L5, 60° ahead and behind Dione, respectively.

Tethys

Tethys or Saturn III is a moon of Saturn, discovered by G. D. Cassini in 1684. This mid-sized moon is about 1,060 km across. It got its name from the Titan Tethys of Greek mythology. Its surface is very bright, making it the second-brightest moon of Saturn after Enceladus and neutral in colour. It has two co-orbital moons, Telesto and Calypso.

Tethys is the third closest of the major moons.

Frozen surface

Like many satellites around Saturn, Tethys is made up of water ice. The frigid surface is highly reflective, a characteristic increased by the shower of water ice particles from the plumes of the moon Enceladus.

Colour patterns

Its surface has many large-scale features distinguished by their colour and sometimes brightness. The trailing hemisphere gets increasingly red and dark as the anti-apex of motion is reached. The leading hemisphere, too, reddens lightly as the apex of the motion is approached, but does not darken.

Odysseus crater

Even though most impact craters are quite small, a giant one known as the Odysseus Crater covers almost two-fifth of the moon's diameter. At 400 km across, it is around the size of Saturn's smallest major moon, Mimas. The crater is quite shallow and its floor conforms to the shape of the moon.

Ithaca Chasma

A large trench runs from the moon's North Pole to its South Pole. It extends up to 2,000 km, spanning almost three-quarters of the planet's circumference. The Ithaca Chasma is 100 km wide and five km deep. The Chasma is believed to be created by the same impact that formed the Odysseus crater. The second cause could be that the surface froze before the core, leading it to expand and crack the crust.

Huge, shallow crater Odysseus, with its raised central complex, the Scheria Montes, is shown at the top of this image.

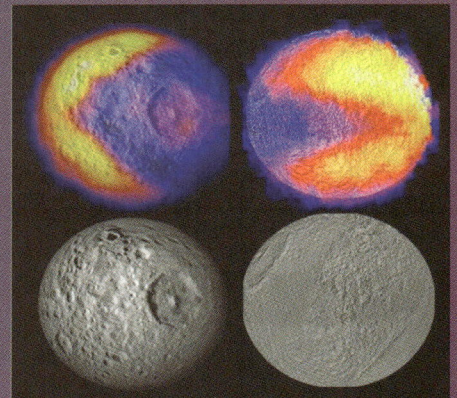

NASA's Cassini spacecraft found a Pac-Man-like shape on Tethys (left).

Tethys pictured along with its planet, Saturn.

Uranian Moons

Uranus is said to have 27 known moons that are divided into three groups. There are five major moons, 13 inner moons and nine irregular moons. The moons are named after characters from the works of Alexander Pope and William Shakespeare.

Uranus and its five major moons.

Uranus

Miranda   Ariel   Umbriel   Titania   Oberon

Inner moons

Uranus is known to hold 13 inner moons. Their orbits lie inside Miranda's orbit. All inner moons are closely connected to the rings of Uranus. The two innermost moons (Cordelia and Ophelia) are known as shepherds, while the small moon (Mab) is a source of Uranus's outermost ring.

Irregular moons

Uranus has nine irregular moons, which orbit at a greater distance than Oberon, the farthest of the large moons. All the irregular moons are thought to be captured objects that were trapped by Uranus soon after its formation. Uranus' irregular moons range in size from 150 km (Sycorax) to 18 km (Trinculo).

A schematic image of the Uranian moon-ring system.

Large moons

The five major moons of Uranus are Miranda, Ariel, Umbriel, Titania and Oberon. Their diameters range from 472 km (Miranda) to 1,578 km (Titania). These moons of Uranus are believed to have been formed in the accretion disc. This existed around Uranus for some time after its formation or resulted from the large impact suffered by Uranus early on.

The skygazers

William Herschel, who discovered the planet of Uranus itself, was the one to discover two of its moons in 1787, Oberon and Titania. William Lassell, an English astronomer, was the one to spot Umbriel as well as Ariel in 1851. Before the space age began, the last moon was discovered by Gerard P. Kuiper in 1948; this was the frankenstein moon, Miranda.

FUN FACT

Caliban, one of Uranus' many moons, moves in an inclined orbit that is opposite to the rotation of Uranus. This shows that it was not formed from Uranus but was a body captured by Uranus' gravity.

Ariel

Of the 27 known moons of Uranus, the fourth-largest, is Ariel (Uranus I).

Ariel rotates and orbits in Uranus' equatorial plane, which is almost perpendicular to Uranus's orbit . For this reason it has an extreme seasonal cycle.

Composition and structure

It is the fourth largest of the Uranian moons. It roughly consists of equal parts water ice and a dense non-ice component, which could be rock and carbonaceous material including heavy organic compounds known as tholins. Given its size and rock and/or ice composition, its interior is divided into a rocky core surrounded by an icy mantle.

Albedo and colour

It is the most reflective of Uranus's moons. Its surface is neutral in colour. The trailing hemisphere appears to be slightly redder than the leading hemisphere. Canyons have the same colour as the cratered terrain.

Geological structures

Its surface can be divided into three terrain types: cratered terrain, ridged terrain and plains. The main surface features are impact craters, canyons, fault scarps, ridges and troughs. The cratered terrain, a rolling surface covered by multiple impact craters, is the moon's oldest and most extensive unit. It is intersected by a network of scarps, canyons and narrow ridges. The longest canyon is Kachina Chasma, at over 620 km in length.

The second main terrain type, ridged terrain, consists of bands of ridges and troughs. Within each band, which can be up to 25 to 70 km wide, are individual ridges and troughs. The newest terrains observed on Ariel, the plains, are relatively low-lying smooth areas. The plains are seen on the floors of canyons and in a few irregular depressions in the heart of the cratered terrain.

▲ Canyons seen on upper left and the prominent noncircular crater below and left of centre is Yangoor.

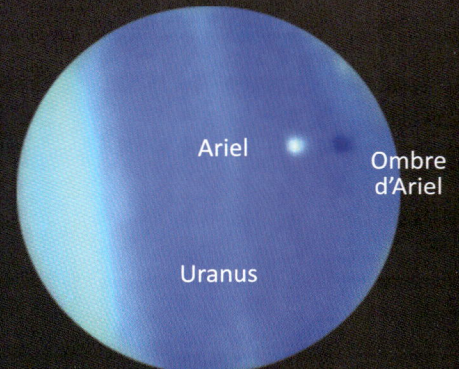

▲ The shadow of Ariel falls on Uranus when it transits through.

Among Uranus's five major moons, Ariel is the second closest to the planet, orbiting at the distance of about 190,000 km.

FUN FACT

Ariel, along with the four major moons, has planetary mass and so would be considered as a dwarf planet if it directly orbited the Sun.

Miranda

The smallest as well as the innermost of Uranus's five round moons is Miranda (Uranus V). Like the other Moons of Uranus, it also orbits in the equatorial plane of Uranus.

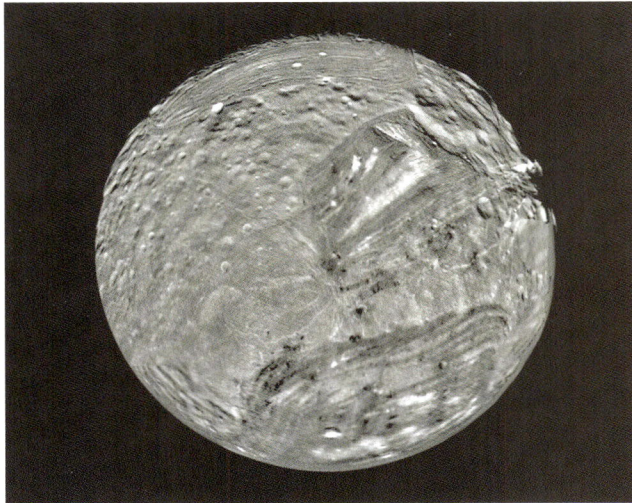

▲ *A close-up of Verona Rupes, the largest known cliff.*

Orbit

Miranda is the only satellite that orbits closest to it, at more or less 129,000 km from the surface. Its orbital period is 34 hours and, like the moon, is synchronous with its rotation period. This means that it always shows the same face to Uranus, a condition known as tidal lock. Its orbital inclination is abnormally high for a body this close to a planet and approximately 10 times that of the other Uranian satellites.

Appearance

Miranda is the least dense of Uranus' round satellites. This suggests a composition of more than 60 per cent water ice. Miranda's surface may be mostly water ice. With the low-density body, it probably contains silicate rock and organic compounds in its interior.

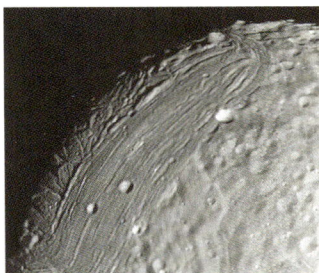

Most of the geological structures on Miranda remain unexplained and are said to be the result of the moon breaking apart and reassembling.

Geological structures

Miranda's surface has mixed regions of broken terrain representing intense geological activity in the past and is criss-crossed by large canyons. It also hosts the largest known cliff in the solar system, Verona Rupes, which has a drop-off of over 5 km. Three giant racetrack-like grooved structures called "coronae" are each at least 200 km wide and up to 20 km deep, named Arden, Elsinore and Inverness. This was discovered on the moon's southern hemisphere. These may have formed via extensional processes at the tops of diapirs or upwelling of warm ice.

Miranda's past geological activity is supposed to have been a result of tidal heating when it was in orbital resonance with Umbriel.

▲ *Uranus along with its five moons.*

At 470 km in diameter, Miranda is one of the smallest objects in the solar system, which is spherical and under its own gravity. ▶

Titania

Titania (Uranus III) is the largest of the moons of Uranus and the eighth largest moon in the solar system. Titania was discovered by William Herschel in 1787. It is named after the queen of fairies in Shakespeare's *A Midsummer Night's Dream*.

▲ *Brightnesswise, Titania lies midway between the dark Oberon and Umbriel and the bright Ariel and Miranda.*

◀ *Comparison of the sizes of Earth, its moon and Titania. Titania is about one-third the size of Earth's moon.*

Orbit

It is the second farthest from the planet among its five major moons. Its orbital period is about 8.7 days. It is synchronised with its rotational period, which means that it is a tidally locked satellite, with one face always pointing towards Uranus. Its orbit lies inside the Uranian magnetosphere; hence, its trailing hemisphere is struck by charged particles, which may have led to the darkening of the trailing hemispheres. This is observed for all Uranian moons except Oberon.

Composition

Titania's much higher density indicates that it consists of almost equal proportions of water ice and dense non-ice components. These could be made of rock and carbonaceous material including heavy organic compounds.

Water ice absorption bands are slightly stronger on the leading hemisphere than on the trailing hemisphere. Besides water, the only other compound identified on Titania's surface is carbon dioxide, which is found mainly on the trailing hemisphere. It is divided into a rocky core surrounded by an icy mantle.

Geological structures

Its surface is generally slightly red. Three classes of geological features are seen on Titania: craters, canyons and scarps. Some craters, for instance, Ursula and Jessica, are surrounded by bright impact rays comprising fresh ice. All large craters on Titania have flat floors and central peaks, except Ursula, which has a pit in the centre.

Atmosphere

The presence of carbon dioxide on the surface suggests that it may have a weak seasonal atmosphere, similar to the Galilean-Jovian moon Callisto.

FUN FACT

There are fewer craters on Titania than on Oberon, which tells scientists that it is actually the younger moon.

Oberon

Oberon, also designated Uranus IV, is the outermost major moon of Uranus. It is the second largest and second biggest Uranian moon. It is also the ninth most massive moon in the solar system. It was discovered by William Herschel in 1787.

Orbit

It is the farthest from the planet among Uranus' five major moons. Its orbital period is around 13.5 days, same as its rotational period. It is a synchronous satellite, tidally locked, showing only one face toward the planet. It spends a significant part of its orbit outside the Uranian magnetosphere. So, its surface is directly struck by the solar wind. Bombardment of magnetospheric particles in objects that orbit inside its magnetosphere leads to the darkening of the trailing hemispheres, which is observed in all of Uranus's moons except Oberon.

Composition and internal structure

Its density is higher than the typical density of Saturn's satellites, indicating that it consists of roughly equal proportions of water ice and a dense non-ice component. Water ice absorption bands are stronger on Oberon's trailing hemisphere rather than the leading one, in contrast to observations on other Uranian moons. It may be differentiated into a rocky core surrounded by an icy mantle.

Geological structures

It is the second-darkest large moon of Uranus after Umbriel. Two classes of geological features are observed on Oberon: craters and canyons. Its surface is the most heavily cratered compared to other Uranian moons. The high number of craters show that it has the most ancient surface among Uranus' moons. The crater diameters go up to 206 km for the largest known crater, Hamlet. Many large craters are surrounded by bright impact rays consisting of fresh ice. Oberon's surface is crossed by a system of canyons, which are less widespread than those found on Titania. The most prominent canyon in Oberon is Mommur Chasma.

▲ *A virtual image of Oberon. The large crater with the dark floor (right) is Hamlet; the crater Othello is to its lower left, and the "canyon" Mommur Chasma is to the upper left.*

▲ *A view of Oberon.*

◄ *Oberon in comparison with Titania.*

FUN FACT

The name Oberon is derived from a mythical king of the fairies, who appears as a character in Shakespeare's *A Midsummer Night's Dream*.

Umbriel

Umbriel (Uranus II) was simultaneously discovered with Ariel. It was named after a character in Alexander Pope's poem *The Rape of the Lock*.

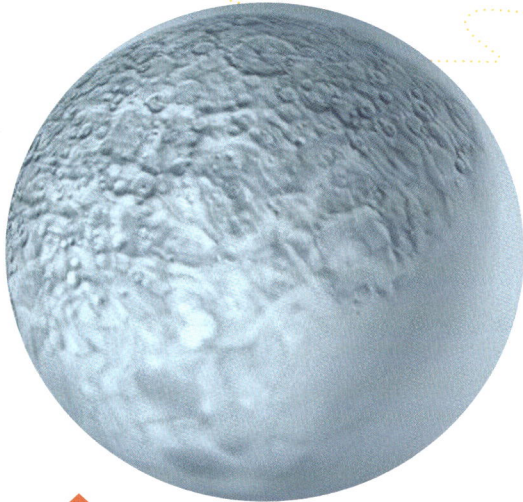

Umbriel's surface is the darkest of the Uranian moons.

Orbit

Umbriel is the third farthest moon from Uranus. Its orbit has a small eccentricity and is slightly inclined towards Uranus' equator. Its orbital period is around 4.1 Earth days; coinciding with its rotational period. Its orbit lies completely inside the Uranian magnetosphere; thus, its trailing hemisphere is struck by charged particles leading to the darkening of the trailing hemisphere. Umbriel also acts as a sink for the magnetospheric charged particles, which creates a pronounced dip in the energetic particle count near its orbit.

FUN FACT

Compared to Ariel, Umbriel only reflects less than half the amount of light. Also, its images show a mysterious bright ring about 140 km in diameter at one of its poles.

Composition and internal structure

Umbriel is the third largest and fourth most massive of Uranian moons. The moon's density indicates that it chiefly consists of water ice, with a dense non-ice component constituting around 40 per cent of its mass. The presence of water ice is supported by infrared spectroscopic observations, which have revealed crystalline water ice on the surface of the moon. Water ice absorption bands are stronger on Umbriel's leading hemisphere than on the trailing hemisphere.

Geological structures

Only one form of geological feature is found on Umbriel-craters. Its surface has several and bigger craters than Ariel and Titania. It shows the least geological activity. The crater diameters range from a few km to 210 km. All recognised craters on Umbriel have central peaks but not rays. The most prominent surface feature is the Wunda crater. It has a diameter of about 131 km and has a large ring of bright material on its floor, which appears to be an impact deposit. Nearby, seen along the terminator, are the craters Vuver and Skynd, which possess bright and tall central peaks.

View of Umbriel from Voyager 1.

Umbriel is a synchronous satellite, with one face perennially pointing towards Uranus.

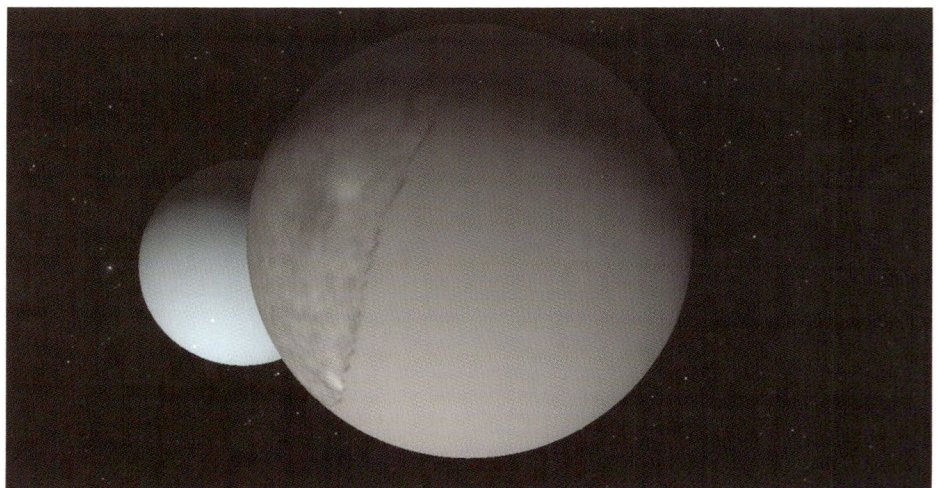

Moons of Neptune

Neptune has 14 known moons. All of these are named after minor water deities in Greek mythology, due to Neptune's position as the god of sea in Roman mythology.

History and background

Triton is the largest of Neptune's moons by far. William Lassell discovered Triton on 10th October, 1846. This is just 17 days after the discovery of Neptune itself. More than a century passed before the discovery of its second moon, Nereid. Neptune's "Nesois" is the moon that orbits the farthest from its planet in the solar system. It has an orbital period of about 26 years.

Characteristics and classification

The moons of Neptune can be categorised into regular and irregular moons. The regular moon group includes the seven inner moons and they follow circular prograde orbits. The orbits lie in Neptune's equatorial plane. The irregular moon group consists of all other moons including Triton. They generally follow inclined, eccentric orbits. These are often retrograde orbits that are far from Neptune. Triton is the only exception to this. It orbits close to Neptune, following a circular orbit. This orbit is still retrograde and inclined.

Regular moons

The regular moons of Neptune are Naiad, Thalassa, Despina, Galatea, Larissa, S/2004 N 1 and Proteus. These are arranged according to increasing distance from the planet. Naiad is the closest regular moon as well as the second smallest among the inner moons. S/2004 N 1 is the smallest regular moon. Prior to its discovery, Naiad was the smallest. Proteus is the largest regular moon as well as the second largest moon of Neptune. The regular moons were probably formed in a place around Neptune.

Irregular moons

The irregular moons of Neptune are Triton, Nereid, Halimede, Sao, Laomedeia, Neso and Psamathe. These are arranged in the order of their increasing distance. The five outer moons of Neptune are similar to the irregular moons of other giant planets like Uranus and Jupiter. They are believed to have been gravitationally captured by Neptune, as opposed to the regular moons.

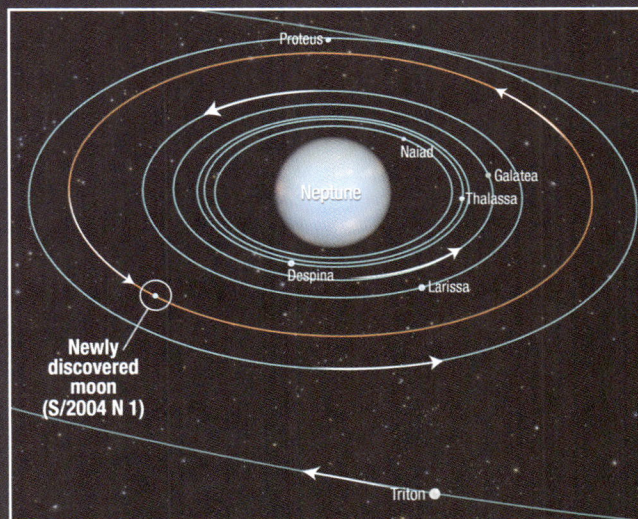

A picture of Neptune and its various moon in their orbits.

A picture of Neptune with its moons.

Triton

Triton is Neptune's largest moon. English astronomer William Lassell discovered it on 10th October, 1846. Triton is one of the very few moons in the solar system known and confirmed to be geologically active.

Discovery

Triton was discovered a mere 17 days after the discovery of Neptune. It is said that when John Herschel received news of Neptune's discovery, he wrote to Lassell suggesting that he search for possible moons of Neptune.

Naming

Triton is named after the Greek sea god Triton, the son of Poseidon. Poseidon is the Greek equivalent of the Roman Neptune. Camille Flammarion initially proposed the name Triton in his 1880 book called *Astronomie Populaire*. It was officially adopted many decades later. Triton was commonly known as "the satellite of Neptune" until the discovery of the second moon about 100 years later.

An artist's impression of Triton. The atmosphere is thin and practically non-existent.

Orbit

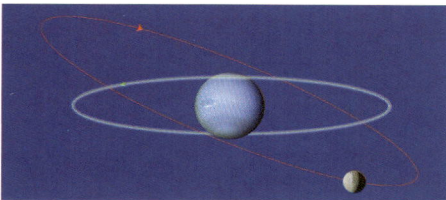

Image showing the orbit of Triton

Triton is unique among all large moons in the solar system. It has a retrograde orbit around its planet. It orbits in a direction opposite to Neptune's rotation. It is worth noting that most irregular moons of Jupiter and Saturn also have retrograde orbits as well as some outer moons of Uranus. However, these moons are all much farther from their planets. They are small compared to Triton. The largest of these moons, Phoebe, has only eight per cent of the diameter and only 0.03 per cent of the mass of Triton.

Capture and atmosphere

Triton was likely "captured" by Neptune. The process would have mostly destroyed the existing satellites into dust and rubble. It has a thin atmosphere of nitrogen and is less than 1000 times as dense as Earth.

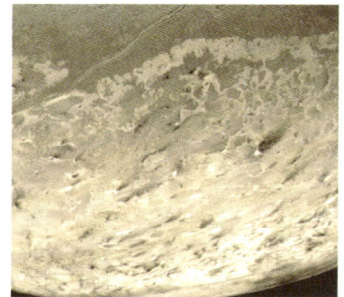

The photo of Triton as taken by Voyager 2.

FUN FACT

Lassell claimed to have also discovered the rings of Neptune. Neptune was later confirmed to in fact have rings. However, they are so faint and dark that it is doubted that he actually saw these rings.

William Lassell discovered Triton after taking Herschel's advice.

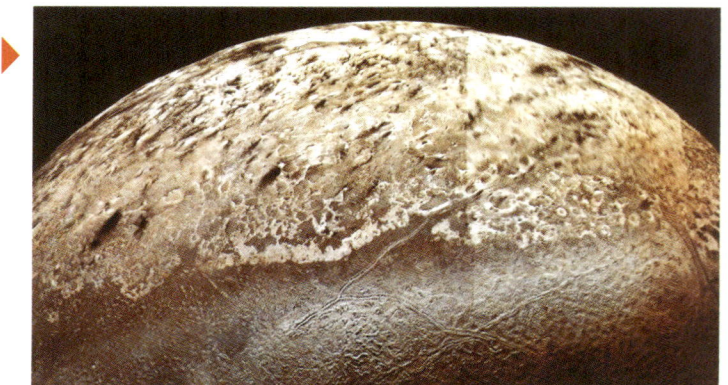

Proteus

Proteus is the second largest Neptunian moon and Neptune's largest inner satellite. It is also occasionally known as Neptune VIII. It is probably not an original body that formed with Neptune. It may have accreted later from the debris that was created when Triton was captured from the Kuiper belt.

Nomenclature and discovery

Proteus was discovered through the images taken by the Voyager 2 space probe two months before its flyby of Neptune in August 1989. It was temporarily designated as S/1989 N 1. Stephen P. Synnott and Bradford A. Smith announced the discovery on 7th July, 1989, with the words "17 frames taken over 21 days". This gives a probable discovery date of sometime around 16th June. On 16th September, 1991, S/1989 N 1 was named after Proteus. It was originally the shape-changing sea god of Greek mythology.

Orbit

Proteus orbits Neptune at a distance that is approximately around 4.75 times the equatorial radius of Neptune. Its orbit is slightly eccentric. It is inclined by about 0.5 degrees to the Neptune's equator. It is the largest of Neptune's regular satellites with a prograde orbit. It rotates synchronously with the orbital motion of Neptune. This means that only one face of Proteus always points to the planet.

Appearance

It is about 420 km in diameter. This makes it larger than Nereid, which was discovered second. Earth-based telescopes did not discover Proteus because it is very close to the planet. Nereid is usually lost in the glare of reflected sunlight from Neptune.

FUN FACT

Proteus is close to a sphere with a radius of about 210 km. The deviations from the spherical shape are large, with the largest up to 20 km in height and crater 15 km deep. Most scientists believe that it is about as large as a body of its density can be, without its own gravity pulling it into a perfect sphere.

Proteus orbiting Neptune: a close-up as taken by the Voyager 2.

Shadow of Proteus on Neptune as seen from another planet.

Nereid

Nereid is Neptune's third largest moon. It has a highly eccentric orbit and is noted for the same. Gerard Kuiper discovered Nereid in 1949. It was, thus, that Neptune's second moon was discovered.

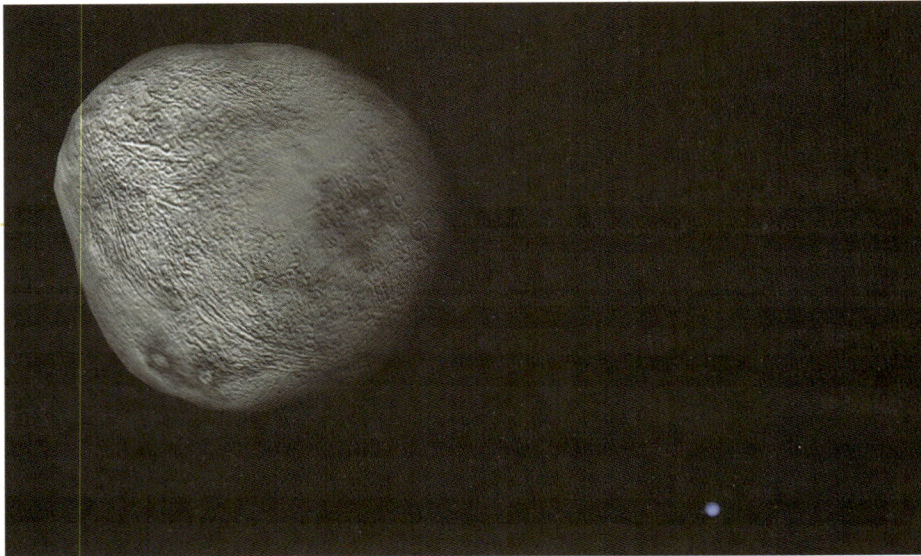

The image of Nereid as captured by Voyager 2 on its fly-by.

Nomenclature and discovery

Nereid was discovered on 1st May, 1949, by Gerard P. Kuiper. He saw it on photographic plates that were taken with an 82-inch telescope by the McDonald Observatory. The name Nereid was mentioned in the report of his discovery. It is named after the Nereids. They were the sea-nymphs of Greek mythology and served as attendants of Neptune.

It was the second and last moon of Neptune to be discovered through Earth-based means. Only after the arrival of Voyager 2 did we make new discoveries.

Appearance

Nereid has an average radius of about 170 km. It is fairly large for an irregular satellite. The shape of Nereid is not known with any certainty. It appears neutral in colour. Astronomers have detected water ice on its surface.

Rotation and revolution

Nereid orbits Neptune in the prograde direction, i.e., in the same direction as Neptune's rotation, at an average distance of 5,513,400 km. However, its highly eccentric orbit takes it as close as 1,372,000 km at its closest point and moves as far as 9,655,000 km at the furthest point.

Theories for eccentricity

The unusual eccentric orbit has three theories:

● it may be a captured asteroid

● it was a Kuiper belt object

● it was an inner moon in the past that was moved into an existing orbit during the capture of Triton.

The phenomena

Astronomers who have observed Nereid over a long period of time have seen a large variation in the brightness of the moon. This happens quite erratically. It is known to happen over a few days, a couple of months or even years! Explorers adhere this change to its extremely elliptical orbit. In fact, there are some astronomers who have not noticed these changes in brightness at all. This means that there is no known pattern to this change and the way it happens is quite chaotic. Astronomers still struggle to explain this phenomena.

FUN FACT

The only spacecraft to visit Nereid has been Voyager 2. It passed Nereid at a distance of 4,700,000 km. This fly-by occurred between 20th April and 19th August, 1989.